The Inside Haircutting System

A Course by Tony Trono

Developmental editing and production management by Janis Fisher Chan.
Design and typography by Christi Payne, Book Arts.
Cover design and drawings by Evana Gerstman, Penngrove, CA.
Drawings on page 2 by Nina Stewart.
Drawings on page 7 by Joshua Fisher.
Cover photograph by Sherrie Blondin.
Photographs by Dale Curtis.
Finished Looks on pages 56–57 by Dale Curtis and Sherrie Blondin.

For information:
Inside Haircutting System Company
765 Baywood Drive, Suite 155, Petaluma, CA 94954
Phone: 707-789-9753
Fax: 707-579-1591
E-mail: tony@trono.com
www.insidehaircuttingsystem.com
ISBN: 0-9715325-0-8

DEDICATION

To my parents, and to Kelly, for believing in me.

CONTENTS

WHY I WROTE THIS BOOK

This book describes the haircutting system I developed after years of searching for a method that would not only allow me to achieve the results I wanted, but let me achieve those results again and again.

Like many hairdressers, I went through a tremendous amount of frustration when I was learning to cut hair. When I asked questions about how to handle specific problems, I received only vague, inconsistent answers. I was left with techniques that sometimes worked, and sometimes didn't. I found it difficult to maintain consistency, or even to remember from one visit to the next how I had achieved a certain style.

What I had been missing was an understanding that a haircut must be supported from the *inside* if it is to hold the outside shape. What I had not realized was that every head has its own unique "map" that—if I followed it— would direct me to the proper divisions on the head so I could distribute the hair properly. What I had not known was that I needed a system to follow, so I could create and recreate specific looks.

When I discovered the Inside Haircutting System, my work took a quantum leap forward. My confidence increased—and so did my client retention and referrals. The hairdressers to whom I have taught this system say the same. Now, through this book, I want to share this system with you.

If you have ever been unable to repeat a haircut that a client "just loved," or if you have felt the frustration of being unable to cut a certain style successfully, I believe that you will find this system as valuable as I do. Whether you are a veteran hairdresser or new to the business, if you are willing to apply yourself, to take the time needed to learn and practice the Inside Haircutting System, you will see the results in improved confidence, and increased business. It's up to you!

—*Tony Trono*

ABOUT THIS SYSTEM

The Inside Haircutting System makes it possible for you to create styles that are compatible for individual clients and recreate those styles again and again. It's a logical, disciplined system in which you start with a specific objective and follow a step-by-step process to achieve it. *The basic steps are always the same*, no matter what style you want to achieve, or how long the client's hair, or whether the hair is curly or straight, coarse or thin.

Benefits of the Inside Haircutting System

We use systems all the time. A system tells us what to do first, what to do next, and so on. Systems reduce problems, increase the chances of achieving our goals, and let us achieve the same results time after time.

Suppose you ordered a jacket from a tailor. To make sure the jacket fit perfectly, the tailor would follow a system: First, decide what fabric to use; next, take careful measurements; then, follow a pattern to cut the fabric; then, baste the seams; and so on. If the tailor skipped key steps, chances are you'd have a jacket you couldn't wear.

In the same way, a pastry chef uses a system to bake a cake. The system specifies what ingredients to use, the order in which to put ingredients together, the type of baking pan, and the cooking time and temperature. If the chef skips steps or does them in the wrong order, the cake probably won't taste very good. Even if it comes out fine, chances are the chef won't be able to replicate it.

Like the tailor and the chef, your work will have better, more consistent results if you follow a system. Here are some of the ways the Inside Haircutting System will help you:

♦ You'll be able to use your haircutting time more efficiently

♦ You'll be able to create fullness and support in the haircuts you do

♦ You'll avoid the mistakes that result from guesswork

♦ You won't need constantly to check and adjust your work

♦ You'll have less difficulty with collapsing areas, such as those behind the ears and at the crown

♦ You'll be able to meet your clients' needs, time and again

How the Inside Haircutting System Works

A good way to understand this system is to think about the process of building a house. When an architect designs the way a house will look, she also needs to design the interior structure that will hold the shape she envisions. The interior structure creates the strength and support that keeps the house from falling down and achieves the look the architect intends.

To create the interior structure for the house, the builder must follow a system: First, construct the foundation; then, add the structural supports; then, raise the walls; and finally, put on the roof. If the architect's structural design is sound and the builder has followed all the steps, the foundation, structural supports, and walls hold up the roof. If the structural design was sloppy or the builder skipped key steps, the structure might collapse.

The beauty of a system for designing and building houses is that once the steps are perfected, the same process and construction techniques can be used to build one house after another. The houses might look very different on the outside, but the structural elements will be very similar.

The same concept applies to creating a fully supported haircut. Think of yourself as an architect and a builder. Your goal is to create the interior structure that will hold the shape you envision. You begin by building a strong foundation. Then you build the structural supports and walls. Finally, you put on the roof. The result is a strong, stable structure that holds the shape of the haircut.

With this system, you start from the bottom and work up and out, creating support from *inside* the haircut itself, not from the outside. You work toward the final shape, instead of starting with the final shape and then going to the interior. It's as if you have a set of construction drawings to follow. If you follow the steps and avoid the temptation to take shortcuts, you'll achieve the results you want.

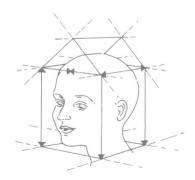

ABOUT THIS BOOK

This book explains and illustrates every step of the Inside Haircutting System. Once you have learned the system, you will be use it to create styles that are compatible for individual clients and repeat those styles consistently by:

- Understanding the ways in which movement, weight, gravity, and stability affect the final look of a haircut
- Moving weight from one area of the head to another
- Stabilizing weight lines
- Creating volume and softness
- Moving smoothly from one stage of the haircut to another

When you begin using this system, you'll notice that the haircut seems to take longer. In fact, it always takes about the same amount of time to complete a haircut. But with this system, you'll use your time differently. You'll spend most of the time actually doing the haircut, cross-checking yourself as you go. Thus, you'll need very little time at the end to check the haircut and hardly any time at all for cleanup.

Here are the steps you'll learn in this book:

Step 1. **What's Your Objective?** What to do at the beginning to make sure that the haircut you're about to create is right for the client.

Step 2. **Sectioning the Hair.** Creating the "map" that tells you where you're going and allows you to cross-check yourself as you work.

Step 3. **Establishing the Baseline (The First Line).** Cutting the line that establishes the maximum length of the haircut.

Step 4. **Cutting the Center Back Section.** Layering and/or graduating to remove or add weight so you can achieve the look you want.

Step 5. **Joining the Center Back to the Side Back Section (The Second Line).** Moving from the center toward the side, continuing to build a strong internal structure for the haircut.

Step 6. **Cutting the Transitional Line (The Third Line).** Joining the back section smoothly to the side section.

Step 7. **Creating the Design Line.** Shaping the haircut around the face.

⌇ NOTE

Learning something new sometimes makes me impatient because it seems to take too long. But I've discovered that frustration is part of the learning process, and that there are no shortcuts to success. Using this system properly takes practice.

To get the results you want, follow the instructions carefully—and practice, practice, practice! As you work, you will see continuing improvement. If you are patient and diligent, you will soon understand how the discipline of the Inside Haircutting System frees you to become increasingly confident in your ability to create and recreate the looks you want.

Step 8. **Cutting the Other Side.** Following Steps 5–7 to cut the hair on the other side of the head.

Step 9. **Cutting the Bang Section and the Top Section.** Finishing the haircut.

Step 10. **Cleaning Up.** With this system, you will have very little cleanup.

BEFORE YOU BEGIN

This book shows you exactly how to use the Inside Haircutting System. Before you begin, read the information below and on the following pages. It provides important background information and explains key features of the system. Pay attention even to information that is familiar, because it might be presented in a new way.

GROWTH PATTERNS AND NATURAL DIVISIONS

The Inside Haircutting System is based on the natural growth pattern (the *terrain*) of the hair and the way the hair naturally divides into sections. The terrain and the divisions give you the information you need to move step-by-step through the haircut.

You will begin an Inside Haircutting System haircut by finding four natural divisions: the **back** section, the **bang** section, and two **side** sections (one on either side of the head). As you work, you will constantly check the divisions and the terrain. They serve as guides, telling you where to go.

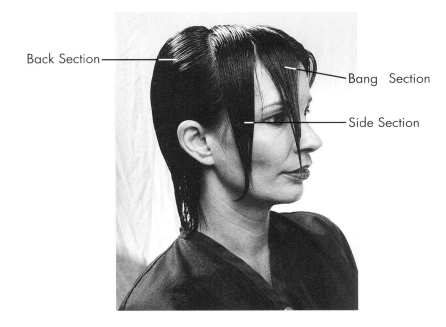

Back Section

Bang Section

Side Section

MOVEMENT, WEIGHT, GRAVITY, AND STABILITY

The system is also based on the four key principles that affect the ability of any hairdresser to achieve specific looks: movement, weight, gravity, and stability.

Movement

The act of setting or keeping in motion.

One way to create a specific style is to force the hair to move in one direction or another. To do that, you need to recognize that movement is determined by hair texture and type of hair. For example, fine, curly hair tends to lift away from the head, while fine, straight hair hangs close to the head. Movement is a factor that determines the volume, so this principle affects the style you can create for a particular client.

Weight

The force of gravity acting on a body.

Weight is determined by the density (number of hairs per square inch), texture (fine, coarse, or medium), and length of hair. Think of the way different kinds of forests look: A redwood forest, with its thick, heavy trees, looks quite different from a birch forest, with light, slender trees. A forest that has been heavily logged is lighter and more open than a dark, dense forest of old-growth trees.

Redwood forest

Birch forest

Like movement, weight affects the look of the hair and may limit the styles you can reasonably create for a particular client. For example, thick, curly hair will bounce right out of a sleek style.

Gravity

The force that tends to draw all bodies in the earth's sphere toward the center of the earth.

Gravity attracts material objects toward the center of the earth. Lift is the process used to oppose, or break free of, gravity. For example, the space shuttle must use great force to break the attraction of gravity that wants to keep it on the ground.

In a haircut, gravity causes weight by forcing hair closer to the head. The more weight hair has, the more it will tend to sit close to the head, and the more graduation and support is needed to create lift.

Stability

The condition of being not easily moved or thrown off balance.

On a shelf, you use bookends to keep a stack of books from falling to the left or right. The 90-degree angles created by the bookends support the books in their upright position. If you remove one angle, the stack will collapse.

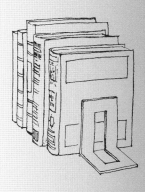

In the same way, 90-degree angles (created by two 45-degree angles) inside the haircut control the movement, support the weight, and create the lift in the hair. Remove the angles, and the hair is likely to collapse.

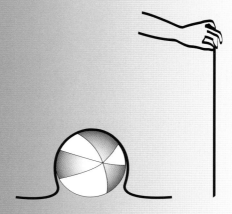

LINES AND CORNERS

With the Inside Haircutting System, you will cut only *straight* lines for the interior structure, never rounded lines. Here's why:

- *It's easier to cut straight lines than rounded lines.* Have you ever tried to cut a circle freehand out of a piece of paper? It's hard to do. It's just as hard to cut round lines when you cut hair. For one thing, you'll find that you round off differently on either side.

- *There's no need to cut round lines.* The rounded shape of the head means that the straight lines you cut appear to become rounded lines. Imagine what would happen if you draped a piece of string on a beach ball. The string, which is a straight line, would appear to become a rounded line. But that piece of string began as a straight line; if you took it off the beach ball and held it up, it would still be a straight line.

- *The corners that result when straight lines intersect trap the weight of the hair and create strength and fullness in the haircut.* This concept is a very important part of the Inside Haircutting System. Think back to the example of building a house. The strongest points in the structure are the corners, which are 90-degree angles created by two 45-degree angles. In the same way, you build corners into the haircut for strength.

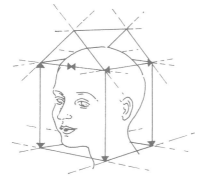

One of the most challenging parts of learning this system is learning to visualize the way the corners work together to trap the hair and create stability in the haircut. After all, the head is round, while corners only exist at the intersection of straight lines.

The corners are created when you cut straight lines first in one direction, then in another. When the lines meet in the correct place, you have an inside corner.

Here's one way to visualize corners. Visualize a box over the client's head. Imagine that the corners in the haircut are connected by straight lines that run diagonally across the box at a 45-degree angle.

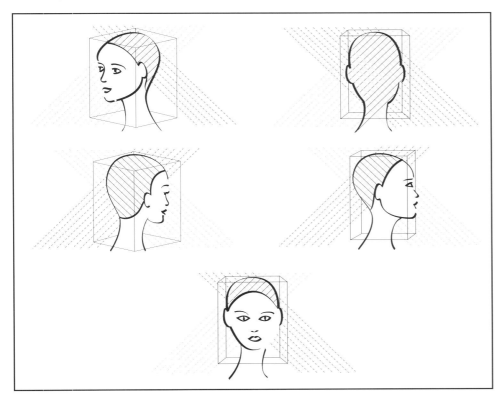

≈ **NOTE**

This might be a brand-new concept for you, very different from the way you learned to think about haircuts. Don't worry if it is not completely clear right now. As you go through this book and practice the system, you will understand how to create inside corners and why they are so important to successful haircuts.

By following this system, you will learn to duplicate corners on the opposite sides of the head. These duplicated corners are what create stability and fullness in the haircut.

PLANES OF THE HEAD

To understand the concept of corners, it helps to think about the planes of the head. You need to create inside corners because you are cutting over different planes.

A plane of the head is the flatter area that lies between curves. The drawing below shows where the planes lie. You will create the inside corners at the intersections of the planes.

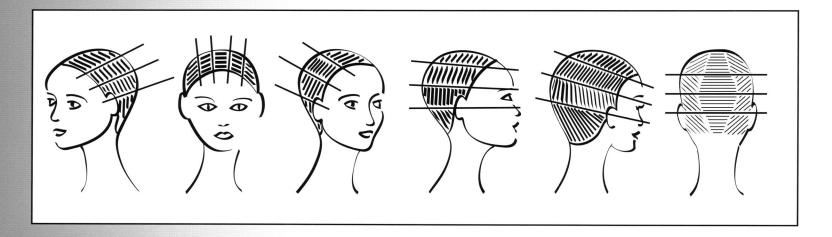

BODY AND HAND POSITIONS

Every tennis player knows that the right body position is crucial to an accurate tennis serve. A guitarist knows that the correct hand position is crucial to playing the right chords. In the same way, how you stand and use your hands when you cut hair affects the outcome of the haircut.

In this book, you'll learn the right body and hand position for each step of a haircut. Here are several important points to keep in mind:

- *Always keep the work directly in front of you.* Move your body as you cut, and use the chair to raise and lower the client to the correct position, so you're always pulling the hair in a flat plane toward the center of your chest. When you're in the correct position, you will be able to cut more evenly and at the right angle. If you need to lean or twist your body because the chair is too high or too low, you will not be able to cut the hair on the right plane.
- *Hold the hair to be cut on the inside of your hand, with the palm facing toward you.* Use your fingers as a guide to cut straight, not curved, lines.

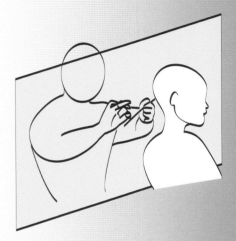

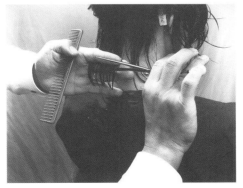

■ *Keep the elbow of the hand that is holding the hair parallel to the line you are cutting.* If your elbow drops down, your line will also drop down.

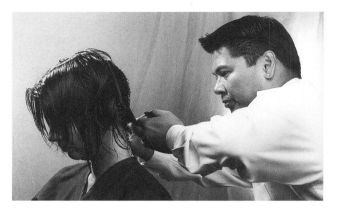

■ *Make sure the hand that holds the hair and the hand that holds the scissors face one another.* We call this hand position "palm to palm."

■ *Move to the hair, instead of moving the hair to you.* When you are too far away from the hair you're about to cut, you'll twist or pull it in an unnatural direction. The hair will buckle and the cut will not be in the place or direction you need it to be.

Wrong: Palm of hand turned up, hair twisted.

SOME IMPORTANT NOTES

- When you first begin using this system, you may notice tension in your arms, hands, and body. That's because you're learning to use different and unfamiliar positions.

  When you become aware of tension, stop for a moment and relax. Shake out your arms and roll your shoulders gently. Repeat as often as needed to keep yourself relaxed. After you've used the new system for awhile, the new positions will be more comfortable, but it's always a good idea to stop working and shake out when you feel tension.

- Stand with your legs slightly apart and your weight evenly balanced. Bend your legs instead of bending at the waist. Think of your body as an elevator, lifting and lowering your arms and hands to the right level. Raise and lower the chair as needed so you can maintain the right body positions more comfortably.

≈ NOTE

Some of the people to whom I've taught this system have had trouble learning this new body position. It does take strengthening your legs so you can use them to support and balance yourself. But the right body position is important because it lets you see your work from the right angle.

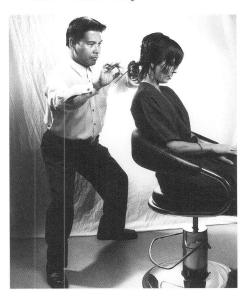

Right: Knees bent and elbows up; chair elevated.

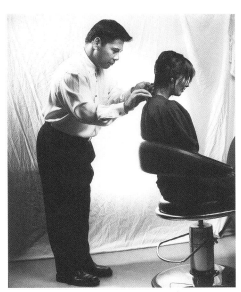

Wrong: Leaning over and bending from the waist; chair too low.

■ As you work, spray the hair as often as needed to keep it moist. It's also important to keep the hair evenly moisturized so the tension remains the same. Lift the hair and spray so you wet all the layers, not only the surface. Spray away from the client's face.

■ Use a comb with medium-wide teeth. Fine teeth compacts and stretches the hair.

THE INSIDE HAIRCUTTING SYSTEM: THE STEPS

STEP 1. WHAT'S YOUR OBJECTIVE?

The first step in the Inside Haircutting System is to make sure that the haircut you're about to create will be compatible with the client's facial structure, type of hair, and patterns of hair growth.

Before shampooing, sit the client in front of the mirror and check the hair. Look at the way it moves, how it falls, and how dense it is. Look for any characteristics that might affect the haircut.

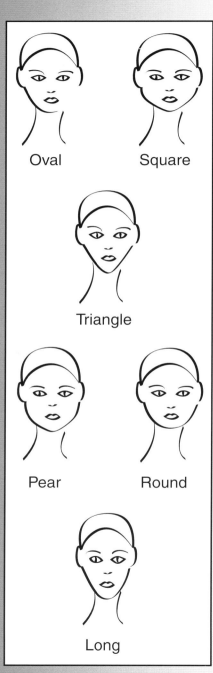

Oval   Square

Triangle

Pear   Round

Long

2. Shampoo the hair. Then comb the wet hair back from the face. Look again at the natural shape of the face and the way the hair falls.

3. Examine the following:
   ♦ the client's facial structure
   ♦ the natural growth pattern of the hair
   ♦ the hairline at the front of the face
   ♦ how the hair lies at the nape of the neck
   ♦ any cowlicks or unusual growth patterns

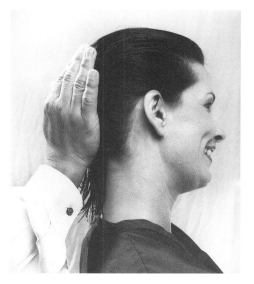

4. Look for the natural part. Comb the hair away from the face. Then put your hand against the head behind the crown and push forward gently.

5. Ask the client about trouble areas. Look closely at the hairline to see how you will need to compensate for individual growth patterns.

6. Visualize the finished haircut. How long will the hair be? How much movement will the style have? Where does the weight need to be to achieve the look you want?

7. If you are working with long hair, cut it straight across to about 1–$1\frac{1}{2}$" below the length the hair will be when you've finished the haircut.

∿ **NOTE**

Be careful not to cut off too much hair. Also, keep the visual image of the finished haircut in mind. But don't worry about achieving it while you follow the steps. The last thing you will do is create the design line, and that's when you will cut off any unnecessary bits.

STEP 2. SECTIONING THE HAIR

To achieve the best results from the Inside Haircutting System, you must section the hair properly. You will create the internal structure for the haircut by cutting each section separately and then joining the sections together.

Before making the first cut, you will divide the hair into four natural sections: the back section, two side sections, and the bang section. The sections create a map that tells you where you're going and allows you to cross-check your work.

To section the hair, you will find the crown reading and the bang reading. It will take some practice to be able to find these readings easily, but it's worth the effort. Sectioning the hair correctly at the beginning of the haircut is the key to achieving your objective.

≋ NOTE

When I read descriptions for doing haircuts, they usually include only a few steps. Sections are approximated. Even in my advanced training, sectioning was explained primarily as a method for getting hair out of the way. In the Inside Haircutting System, we use precise sectioning, as dictated by the head itself, to create support and make it possible to duplicate the haircut time and again.

Finding a true crown reading

The crown is the highest point on the head. All the hair on the head falls from the crown. You can think of the crown as the distribution point—the point from which all the hair is distributed.

The crown reading tells you which hair belongs in the **back** section—the hair that falls naturally behind the crown. It is important to take the crown reading correctly so the hair will be distributed from the right point. Otherwise, the weight will be distributed incorrectly and the haircut will collapse.

Here's how to find a true crown reading:

1. Stand in front of the client's shoulder, with your body facing the shoulder. Be careful not to stand behind the shoulder, because you'll have to twist your body, which will make it difficult to find the true crown reading.

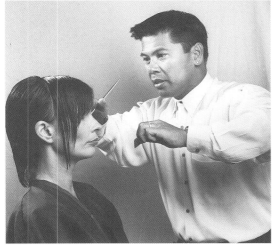

Right

Wrong

~~~ **REMINDER**

Keep the work in front of you.

THE INSIDE

≋ **NOTE**

Many haircut descriptions illustrate sectioning across the top of the head just behind the ears. I have found this method to be very dangerous. Without the true crown reading, the weight distribution and stability will be compromised.

2. Comb the hair in the direction it grows naturally—its natural growth pattern. Remember to use a comb with medium-wide teeth.

3. Take about an inch of hair from the temple area between the front edge of the ear and the corner of the eye. Hold the hair between your forefinger and thumb or forefinger and knuckles. Gently push the hair straight up toward the crown, or the top of the head. The hair will automatically divide from the middle of the temple up to the true crown.

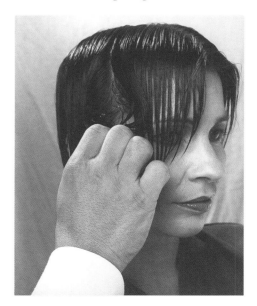

4. Comb the hair back from the point at which it divides. Let the hair in front of the dividing point fall forward, or comb it forward and clip it away.

5. Repeat on the other side. Don't try to make the sections line up on both sides.

≈ **NOTE**

This process takes practice. Every head structure and hair growth pattern is different, so it's important to practice finding the correct readings.

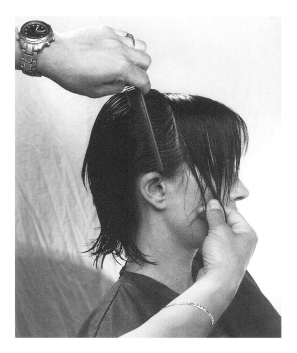

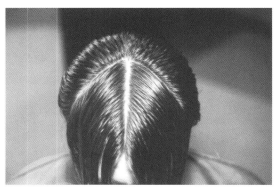

Right

As you work, keep the following in mind:

- Be careful not to force the hair. Simply lift it and let the head tell you where to go.
- Once you've found the true crown reading, the hair will actually come to a V at the top of the head. The true crown is at the point of the V.

Finding the bang reading

1. Keeping the back section combed or clipped away from the face, comb the remaining hair forward and let it fall naturally over the forehead.

2. Standing in front of the client, take a one-inch section of hair at eyebrow level and push it up gently, first on one side, then on the other. The hair will divide to give you the bang reading. Clip the bang section up and out of the way.

Now you have four sections:

- **The back section,** which is all the hair that falls behind the V created by the crown reading

- **The bang section,** which is all the hair that falls between the two lines created by the bang reading

Back Section —————— Bang Section

Side Section

- **Two narrow "side" sections,** one above each temple, which is the hair that remains after you have sectioned off the back section and the bang section

STEP 3. ESTABLISHING THE BASELINE (The First Line)

No matter what type of haircut you are doing or what look you want to achieve, you will almost always begin by establishing a baseline at the back of the head. The baseline is the first of the three lines that will create a corner.

The baseline establishes the maximum length of the haircut. The baseline is a straight line that is even on both sides of the back of the head.

Depending on the look you want, you will cut the baseline below, on, or above the hairline. For example, if you're doing a graduated haircut, you might cut the baseline on or above the hairline.

Here's how to do it:

1. Stand directly behind the client, facing the back of the client's head. Be sure to

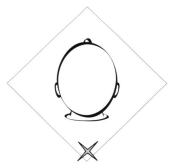

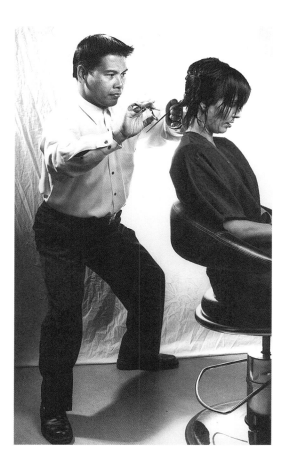

keep your elbows parallel with the line you are cutting.

2. Divide the hair in the back section into a right section and a left section. The sections will be on either side of the line that runs from the crown down the middle of the head to the nape of the neck.

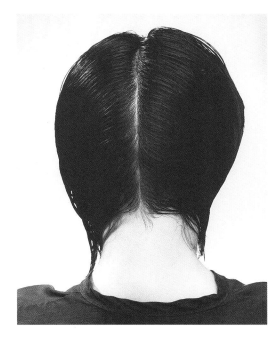

3. Taking hair from both the right and left sections, comb a subsection straight down toward the nape. Be sure to comb the hair in its natural growth pattern. Clip the rest of the hair up and out of the way.

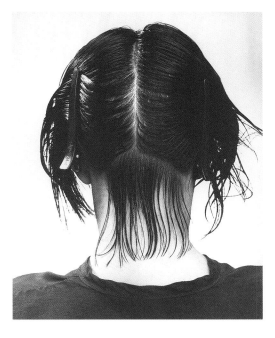

≈ BODY POSITION

Keep the elbow of the hand that's holding the hair at a level with the line you are cutting. If your elbow drops down, the line also drops down. If necessary, raise the chair so you can keep your elbows up. The elbow of the hand that's holding the scissors should also be up.

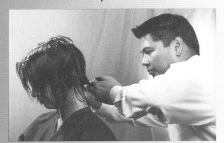

Right

Wrong: Elbows dropped.

4. Now cut that subsection. Take about an inch of hair from the center of the subsection between your forefinger and middle finger. The palm of your hand should face your chest. Gently pull the hair straight down. Following the growth pattern, pull straight down, not to the side, and be sure to hold the section of hair so it does not twist or buckle.

Wrong: Palm of hand turned up, hair twisted.

Right: Palm of hand facing slightly down, hair not twisted.

5. Using your finger as a guide, cut the hair straight across. Cut only what you can easily handle.

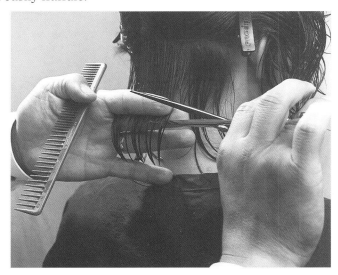

OPTION: Lifting the hair away from the head before cutting it will give you a soft line. For a more solid line, you can cut the hair against the skin of the neck, as shown below.

6. Repeat the process, pulling out some of the hair that you have already cut to use as a guide. Cut the right subsection first, and then the left, or vice versa, until you have cut a straight (180-degree) line at the maximum length you want the hair to be. Continue to cut until you run out of hair. (Imagine a subsection of hair that goes on into infinity that you could continue to pull down and cut.)

≈ **NOTE**

Move as often as necessary to keep the work directly in front of you. Your line will droop slightly at the sides—don't worry about it. You'll take care of it later. To avoid rounding the line, move your body in a straight line from side to side as you make each cut.

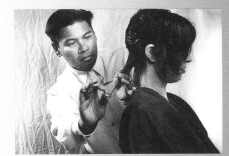

Wrong: Not directly behind work.

STEP 4. CUTTING THE CENTER BACK SECTION

The way you cut the center back depends on the type and density of the hair and the look you want to achieve.

Unless you doing a one-length haircut, in which you cut all the hair to the length of the baseline, your next step will be to **layer** and/or **graduate** the hair.

- **Layering** removes weight from the back section of the hair. When you layer the hair, you cut it to meet an imaginary perpendicular wall—in other words, you cut a line that runs straight up or straight down.

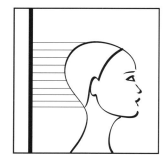

- **Graduating** adds weight to the back section of the hair. When you graduate the hair, you cut it to meet an imaginary line that runs at a 45-degree angle up from the nape of the neck.

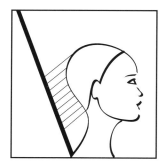

≈ NOTE

For some haircuts, you will do a combination of graduation and layering. You will first cut the hair to meet an imaginary line running at a 45-degree angle up from the nape of the neck. Then you will cut it to meet the imaginary perpendicular wall.

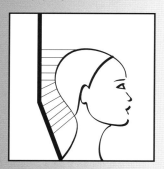

Keep in mind

- Begin at the center of the back of the head. Move first from the center to the right or the center to the left. Move from side to side with each cut.

- Make sure your body faces the work. Cut the hair to meet the imaginary wall at the center of your chest.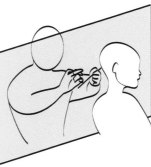

- Work with a 1" or $1^1/2$" subsection at a time. Complete the entire center back section before moving to the side back sections. Be sure not to take hair from the side sections.

- As you pull out sections of hair, check the terrain. Look at the direction in which the hair grows naturally out of the head. Be sure to pull the hair in that direction, and not to force it into an unnatural direction. Cut only the amount of hair you can easily handle at one time.

- Keep all layers of the hair moist.

∿ NOTE

As you work, visualize the finished haircut. But remember, you are still cutting the *internal* structure. You will create the design line and clean up uneven spots later.

Layering the hair

Layering removes weight from the hair, so be sure the baseline has enough weight before you begin layering. For a heavier line, you may need to cut two or three sections to establish the baseline before you start layering.

Here's what to do:

1. Move about 1" up the head. Take down another subsection from the right side of the head and clip the rest away. Repeat on the left side. Take an even amount of hair from both sections.

   OPTION: If the hair is very dense, skip Step 1 and go on to Step 2, where you will begin the layering process by taking the first vertical section from the center of the baseline.

2. Still standing behind the client, take a small vertical section from the hair at the center of the back of the head between your fingers. The section should include hair from both the right and the left subsections. Pull the hair straight back toward you on a vertical plane. Let some of the hair drop out of the section to the baseline, and start layering above it.

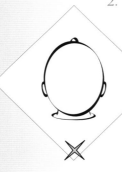

Notice the hair dropping out— that's how you know that you're not cutting off the baseline.

3. Gently pull the vertical section straight toward the imaginary wall in front of the middle of your chest. Using your fingers as a guide, cut the section straight up or straight down until you run out of hair.

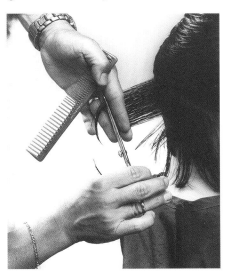

≋ REMINDER

If you are right-handed, the chair will be low when you are cutting the right side. Raise the chair when you cut the left side.

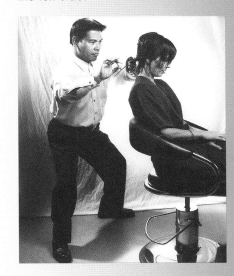

4. Moving up the back of the head, take down another vertical section and comb it down. Cut it to the line of the previous section.

5. Continue moving up the head to the crown, cutting each new line to the line of the previous sections. Move up only as far as the crown. Imagine a line jutting out from the top of the head. The last section should be no higher than that line.

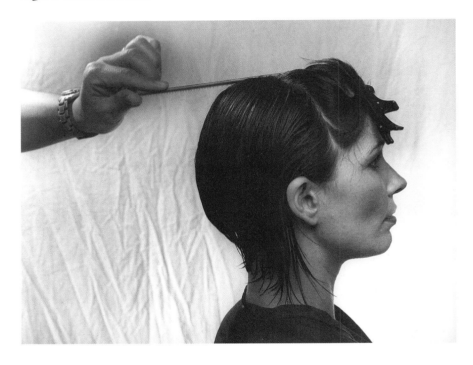

REMINDER

Depending on whether you're working on the right or left side, your fingers will point straight up or straight down. If your fingers point down, your elbow will point up, and vice versa.

CAUTION: Don't cut off the extra bits on the sides or you will round the line. You'll take care of those bits later.

Graduating the hair

To create a weight line that creates fullness in the haircut, graduate the back section of hair up to the crown. For a softer hairline, begin the graduating process earlier.

You can create a graduated line on a horizontal plane or at an angle. Horizontal lines tend to leave the hair heavier, while lines cut on a diagonal tend to reduce weight.

When you begin graduating you will usually cut the hair on a horizontal plane. As you move up the head from a short layer to a longer layer, the angle can get steeper, depending on how much graduation you want, until you are cutting at a 45-degree angle across the back of the head.

⁓ BODY POSITION

As the angle gets steeper, your body and arm position will change. When cutting the right side of the back section, your left elbow will be up and your right elbow will be down.

Of course, when you cut the left side of the back section, you will reverse this body and arm position. Your right elbow will be up and your left elbow will be down.

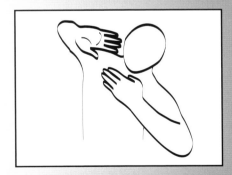

Here's what to do:

1. Comb another horizontal section down toward the baseline, taking the hair from both the right and left subsections at the center back of the head.

2. Lift the horizontal section and gently pull it straight toward the imaginary wall at the center of your chest. With your palm facing your chest, and using your thumb and forefinger as a guide, cut the section so it is a bit higher than the baseline. Cut straight across. To keep an even tension in the hair, don't cut past the second digit of the finger that is holding the hair.

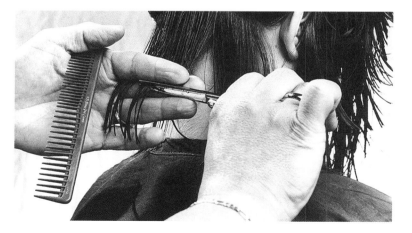

3. When you've finished cutting the first section, bring down another $\frac{1}{2}$"-1" section. Repeat the process, cutting a little higher than the previous line. Continue moving up the head, graduating one section at a time, until you reach the top of the head. The line will become increasingly diagonal, depending on how much graduation you need to create.

〰 NOTE

In the photos, notice the angle of the hand and the hair that is being held. The hair is not being lifted higher than the sections allow. If you do lift the hair higher, you will begin to layer it.

Here's an example of what the hair will look like when you've finished graduating it. Notice how the baseline appears to curve, even though you have been cutting only straight lines.

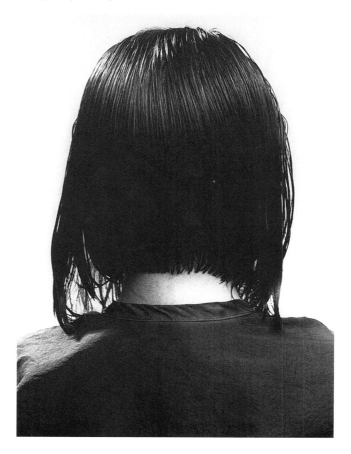

STEP 5. JOINING THE CENTER BACK TO THE SIDE BACK SECTION (The Second Line)

After you've finished cutting the center back section, you need to join the center back to the side back section. When you do this, you will create the second of the three lines that form a corner.

You are still working only with the **back** section, the distribution of hair behind the crown. After this step, you will cut the transitional line to blend the side section to the back section, and then you will create the design line.

For now, however, you will leave the side section clipped up and out of the way.

Complete the following three steps on one side of the head before moving to the other side.

Here's what to do:

1. If necessary, let the side section down and take another crown reading. Clip the side section away.

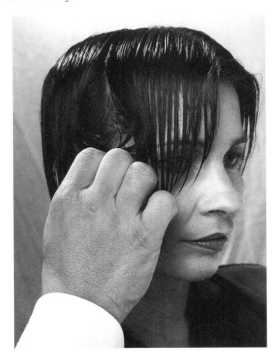

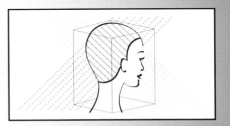

≈ REMINDER

You are still cutting only straight lines, continuing to build a strong internal structure for the haircut.

THE INSIDE

NOTE

If the hair is very short, you will start lower down toward the middle back of the ear, instead of toward the top.

REMINDER

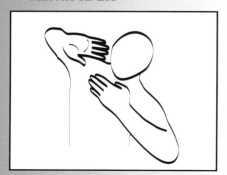

You are cutting from low to high. Check your body position. If you are right-handed, your left elbow should be lower than your right.

2. Comb down a section from the top of the ear toward the center back at a diagonal. Clip the rest of the hair in the section away. You will see a line running at an angle from the top of the ear toward the center back of the head.

3. Stand behind the client's shoulder with your body facing the side back section. Pull a section of hair toward the imaginary wall at the center of your chest. Be sure to pull the hair in the direction it grows naturally out of the head. Watch for buckling or twisting that indicates you are lifting the hair too high or forcing it in an unnatural direction.

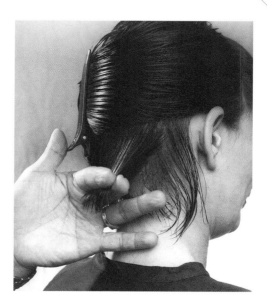

4. With your fingers and the scissors at the same angle as the line running from the ear toward the nape of the neck, cut a straight line to the length of the shortest hair in the section. Cut first from the center to the right and then from the center to the left (or vice versa). Be sure to follow the growth pattern of the hair.

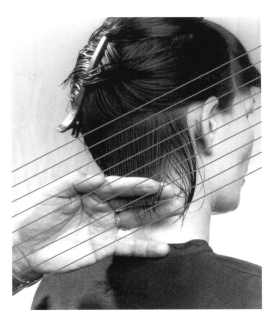

5. Moving toward the ear, pull out another section, and cut it. Continue toward the ear until you run out of hair.

~ **NOTE**

The fingers in this picture are actually held correctly. It is the curvature of the head that makes them appear to be at a different angle than the lines.

~ **NOTE**

Notice that the angle of the section appears to curve according to the shape of the head. Remember the string and the beach ball? The string appears to curve when it takes on the shape of the ball.

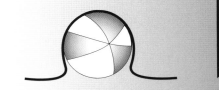

6. Comb down another section
and repeat steps 4 and 5.
Continue moving up the head,
always working from the
center to the ear, until you
have taken all the hair down
from the crown and cut it.

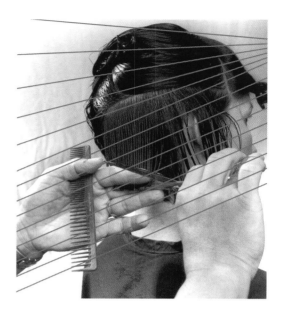

As you move up the head, the line
will change, becoming flatter,
then appear to curve, then
become more angled again,
depending on the plane. Always
use that line as a guide to determine the angle of the cut.

As you work, you can see the
graduated line. Notice how the
straight lines you cut create a
rounded shape, because of the
rounded shape of the head.

When you're finished, you will
have joined the center back to the
side back. Don't worry about the
scraggly bits and pieces; you'll
clean them up later.

STEP 6. CUTTING THE TRANSITIONAL LINE (The Third Line)

The transitional line joins the back side section to the side section. This is the third line that creates the corner. Complete the transitional line and the design line on one side of the head before moving to the other side.

Here's how:

1. Stand with your body facing the client's shoulder. Take the side section down and comb it into the back section.

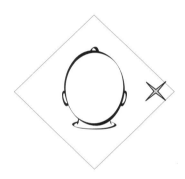

2. Take another crown reading and comb the side section away for the moment. Imagine a line that runs from the middle of the forehead back to the occipital area. Take the remaining hair from the side back section above the imaginary line and clip it away.

≋ BODY POSITION

Cut the hair at a 45-degree angle from down to up or up to down, depending on which side you are cutting. Keep your elbows on a 45-degree plane.

≋ REMINDER

As you work, continue to check the terrain. Look at the direction in which the hair grows naturally out of the head, and be sure to pull the hair in that direction. Be careful not to force the hair into an unnatural direction.

≈ **NOTE**

Find the short pieces from the side back. Use them as your guide.

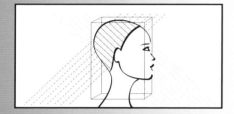

3. Take a diagonal section from the side back section slightly above the ear. This line is parallel to the crown reading. Pull the hair out at a 45-degree angle. Using your finger as a guide, cut the hair in a straight line to the length of the shortest hair in the section.

4. Moving forward toward the temple, take another section of hair and cut it.

5. Comb down another section and cut it to the previous line. Repeat, moving up the head to the crown. Be careful not to lift the hair higher than the top of the head.

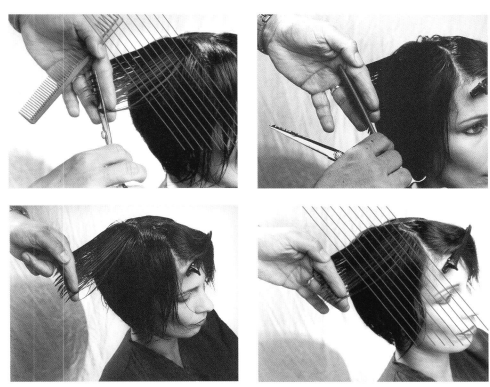

STEP 7. CREATING THE DESIGN LINE

When you cut the design line, you accomplish two things: You continue the process of joining the back section to the side section, and you determine the way the haircut will look around the face. The length at which you cut the design line, and whether you cut it on a horizontal or diagonal plane, depends on the look you're going after. Below are some ideas.

Design Lines

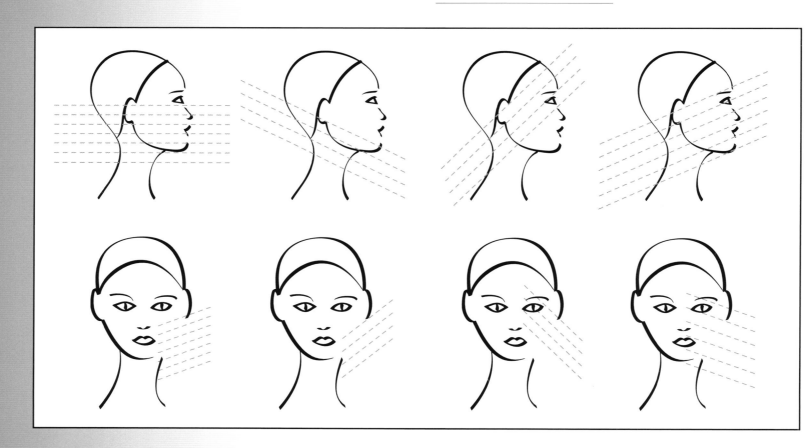

Here's how to create the design line:

1. If necessary, section off the bangs again. Unclip the bang section and take another bang reading, just as you did at the beginning of the haircut. Then clip the bang section away again.

2. Find the crown reading again. If necessary, comb the back section (the hair behind the crown reading) away.

   CAUTION: You create the design line in the side section. Be careful not to comb hair from the side section into the back section.

3. Just as you did at the beginning of the haircut, step back and look at the client in the mirror. Once again, visualize the look of the finished haircut.

≋ **REMINDER**

Keep your eyes level to the section you're working on, and imagine a straight line running from your elbow through your scissors and your fingers. If you need to be lower, lower the chair or bend from the knees. Resist the temptation to bend from the waist; you won't be able to see the line you're working on. Also, keep the growth pattern of the hair in mind. Do not twist the hair or pull it in an unnatural direction.

≋ BODY POSITION

The nature of the design line will determine your elbow position. If you're cutting from short to long, your right elbow will be up and your left elbow will be down.

If you're cutting a parallel line, your elbows will be parallel.

If you're cutting an A line, your left elbow will be up and your right elbow will be down.

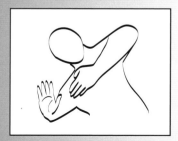

4. Stand in front of the client's shoulder, with your body facing the shoulder, so that you are standing directly in front of the hair you are about to cut. Working only with the amount of hair you can handle easily, subsection the side section and clip the remaining hair up.

5. Cut the subsection to create the design line. Using your finger as a guide, cut straight lines, continuing to cut until you run out of hair.

6. Drop the next section down and repeat, moving up the head until you've cut all the hair in the side section.

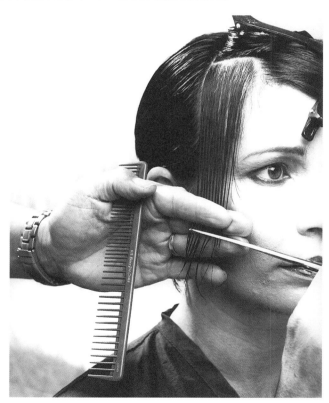

7. Next, you will join the side section to the side back section. Once again, subsection the side section that you have just cut. Clip the subsection up, just as you did in Step 4.

8. Comb a subsection of the side back section down and into the side section. Clip the rest of the hair up. Using the side section as the guide, cut the hair in the side back section to match the design line. Move from front to back until you have cut all the hair in that section.

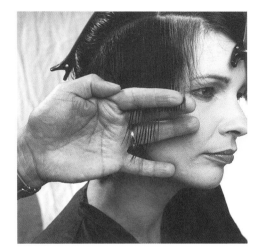

9. Take down another section from the side and back sections and repeat until you reach the crown.

STEP 8. CUTTING THE OTHER SIDE

You have now cut the hair on one side of the head. Follow Steps 5, 6, and 7 to join the center back to the side back section, cut the transitional line, and create the design line on the other side.

Begin by checking the sectioning again. When you comb down the first section, check the client's face in the mirror. Be sure to create the design line on the same level as on the other side.

≋ **NOTE**

When I first learned to cut hair, I was often taught to create the design line when I began the haircut, and then work within that shape. The difficulty I found was in creating internal support for the haircut without affecting its shape. When I developed the Inside Haircutting System, I realized that it's much more logical to build the internal support first, and then create the design line. Remember—when you build a house, you create the support before you finish the outside shape.

STEP 9. CUTTING THE BANG SECTION AND THE TOP SECTION

The last part of the haircut is to cut the bang section and the top section.

Cutting the bang section

1. Standing in front of the client, comb the bang section down and find the bang reading again.

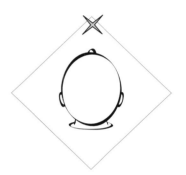

2. Comb down a subsection and clip the rest of the hair away. Cut the subsection to the length you want. Continue to pull down the subsections and cut them until you run out of hair.

 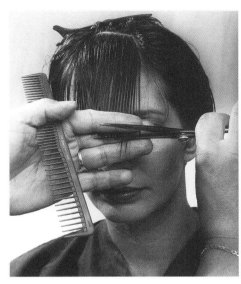

3. Join the bang section to the side section. Working first on one side of the head and then the other, comb the bang section into the side section. Cut the line as needed. Be sure to cut straight lines. Whether you cut the lines at a horizontal or diagonal angle depends on the look you want to achieve.

THE INSIDE

Cutting the top section

The top section is the circle of hair in front of the crown.

1. Find the crown reading on both sides of the head.

2. Standing directly behind the client, pull a section from the crown straight up. Using the short pieces of hair as your guide, cut the hair in a straight line.

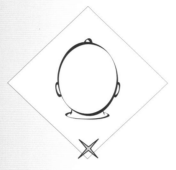

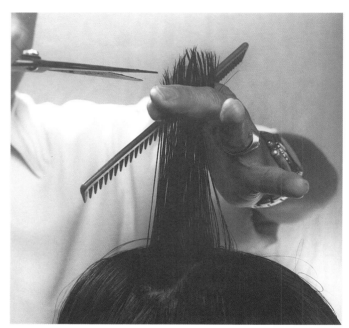

≋ NOTE

Make sure your elbows are up. If your elbows drop, your line will drop.

3 Lift another section up, pulling in a little hair from each of the side sections. Cut to the same length as the first section.

3. Moving forward toward the face, continue until the top section is the length you want it to be.

STEP 10. CLEANING UP

With the Inside Haircutting System, this step isn't much of a step because there's very little cleanup. You might need to clean up a line or clean up around the ears. When you blow-dry the hair, you might clean up the neck a little. That's it.

THE NINE CORNERS

Here are the nine corners you have created to support the haircut, using the Inside Haircutting System:

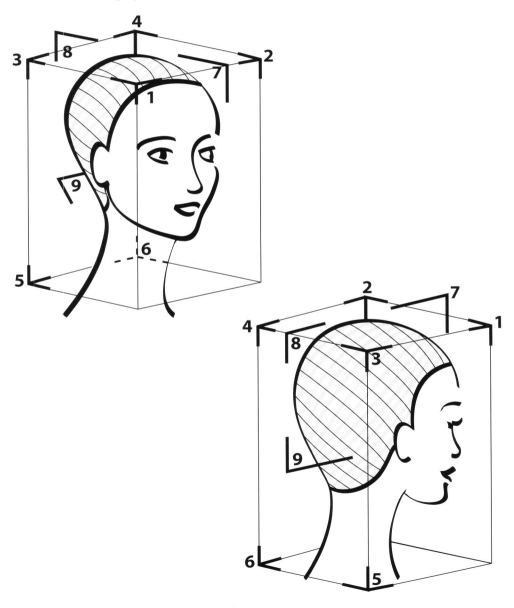

FINISHED LOOKS

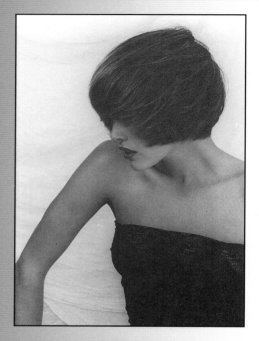

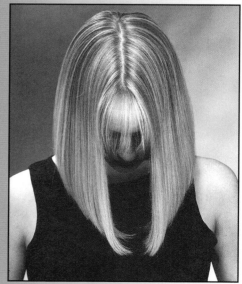

FINISHED LOOKS

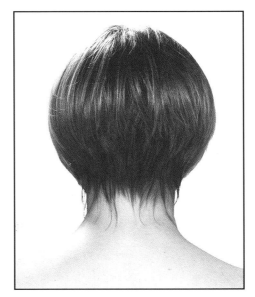

TO ORDER ADDITIONAL BOOKS

To order the *Inside Haircutting System*, complete this form and send it to us at the address below. Include your credit card number and expiration date or a check for $29.95 plus $3.50 to cover shipping and handling (CA residents add applicable sales tax).

Name: _____

Address: _____

_____ zip code

Tel: ( ) _____

Fax: ( ) _____

E-mail: _____

☐ Please charge my credit card   ☐ I've enclosed a check

Credit card # _____

Expiration Date _____

Signature _____

You can also order this book on our Web site:
www.insidehaircuttingsystem.com

Please contact us for information about discounts for schools and resellers.
Inside Haircutting System
765 Baywood Drive, Suite 155
Petaluma, CA 94954

Tel: 707-789-9753   Fax: 707-579-1591
E-mail: tony@trono.com
www.insidehaircuttingsystem.com